DARK ON ME

DARK ON ME

Published by
Amethyst Quill Publishing
ISBN: 979-8-9986191-3-7

7326 • 7826

For inquiries or permissions, contact:
such.small.hands1307@gmail.com

To my beautiful *Stargirl*—

You are in every page,
the silence between the lines,
and every reason
I keep writing.

This book is dedicated to
those who carry the fire
through what was taken,
what remains,
and what rises.

Where Darkness First Falls

Some of these poems were written when I was a teenager, while I was surviving things I did not yet have the language for. Others followed over the years, as life made its lessons unmistakable. They were written in love and loss, faith and doubt, beauty and wreckage. They were written because silence was no longer an option.

There were seasons when I clung to God, and one when I let go. I have believed deeply and walked away angry. I have prayed through tears and sat in the silence between my prayers and God's answer, wondering if anyone was listening. Even then, something in me kept reaching.

This book is for anyone who grew up too fast, carried more than they could say, or gave too much of themselves away. It is for anyone who loved deeply and paid for it.

The poems, written over many years, became a record of my life. They do not soften what was hard, nor do they exaggerate what was good. They simply tell the truth. Emotions may have amplified these words, and time may have distilled them, but they are still mine.

Maybe you are trying to remember who you were before the world told you who to become. Maybe you are still becoming.

Either way, I hope these pages make room for your story, too.

CONTENTS

SECTION I: HANDS LIKE HOUSES

SECTION II: THE UNINVITED

SECTION III: SMOKE & MIRRORS

SECTION IV: ELECTRIC NIGHTS

SECTION V: DYING TO LOVE

SECTION VI: FORGED

this is

dark on

me.

I
HANDS LIKE HOUSES

the dark no longer frightens me.

it has walked beside me
long enough to feel like company.

sometimes

it drapes across my shoulders
like a tattered coat.

Disturbed

I keep things in order,
corners undisturbed,
damage I've learned to explain away.

I speak softly,
like I'm trying not to wake something.

I wait for someone
long enough
to notice how I shut down
when I feel too seen.

When someone finally stays,
I start counting the days.

what a strange thing

to be here

but not here.

to slip between moments

unnoticed.

Taken Under

Solitude became
my only shelter.

I didn't want to be alone.
I wanted protection.

I built it high enough
so no one could reach me.

A self-inflicted exile,
meant only to keep me
from being taken under.

Sleight of Hand

It is the nerve
that remembers touch.

I know what it means
to be claimed before consent.

Years slipped through me,
unmarked on the outside.

I did not shatter loudly.
I thinned.

But
I am still here,
not whole,
not new,
permanently altered.

Class of 2001

I skip meals
and call it discipline.
Wearing oversized hoodies,
not for comfort
but to hide the body
I learned to hate.

I stand in a room
where everyone seems to belong,
except me.

It is the careful smile
when someone compliments me
and then the slow dismantling
in the car afterward.

sadness cries.

sadness spills.

depression settles.

She Seemed Happy

Sometimes I miss the cruelty,
because at least when they hurt me,
I knew I existed.

They all say they didn't know:
That I seemed happy,
always smiling.

I smiled
so they wouldn't ask.

Human

It is embedded
in the rituals of the day:

"Don't eat that.
You don't deserve to feel full."

"Don't look at yourself.
There will always be something else
to dislike."

You begin to believe
that your presence
is an apology.

It is getting dressed
without looking in the mirror,
only to find yourself there anyway.

Skyscraper

I built myself with precision.
An architecture of defense.

They call me strong,
but it is armor.

When I wanted to call,
the moment froze.
When I needed to speak,
I convinced myself
it wasn't worth saying.

I would open my phone
only to close it.

Not because no one was there,
but because I had already decided
they wouldn't care.

i fluttered between

irrational hope

and calculated withdrawal.

sometimes

i trace the walls

unsure if

i built them

or they built me.

detachment does not erase
it distorts.

no bridges were burned
only wraiths
waiting to be faced.

To a Lonely Room

Loneliness begins
as a feeling.

At first
it is a wound.

You notice it.
You speak of it.
You wait for it to pass.

But time is patient.

A scar forms
around the emptiness.

And one day,
without realizing it,
loneliness is no longer
something you feel.

It becomes
a way of being.

Killing Strangers

I walk into rooms
and forget why I came.

The lights are on,
but nothing answers.

They say,
"Just find yourself,"
as if it were that simple.

I perform life
like I'm auditioning for it.

there are moments
i reach for what is familiar
before i become
something unrecognizable.

i did not choose this.

i carried

many versions of myself.

i kept waiting

to meet

the real one.

Change

Some days, I am the spring.
As if the world
has finally made sense.

Then the air shifts.
There is a familiar presence
just beyond my reach.

The change in my voice,
the pause between words,
the way my thoughts pace.

Some days, I search
for the self I remember.
Other days, I learn
to accept the one that arrives.

A Ghost Wearing My Things

I am tired.
Tired in a way
that makes dreams feel irrational.

The dread is already here,
in the rise of my chest.

The way I flinch
when someone
turns toward me.

Fear of entering a room
and being watched
a moment too long.

Fear of being excessive.
Fear of being nothing.

i wear many faces
a gallery of borrowed expressions.

some rise like floodwater
pressing against my bones
prisoners remembering sunlight.

the others stand behind my eyes
breathing in the dark.

this is what it's like

to live inside me.

Zombie

People think
suicide is about death.

But for me
it is about quiet,
about wanting
the war in my head
to lay down its weapons,
about wanting to rest.

I've been surviving
longer than I've been living.

I don't want a funeral.
I want relief.

Hands Like Houses

My hands became houses.
Doors remain open,
but the hinges remember every slam.

Wounds wrapped carefully,
not in bandages
but in gift paper
so no one feels guilty holding them.

I empty myself
like bottles left near the edge of a table,
waiting to be knocked over.

I have stood at the brink of leaving.
Bare feet on splinters
of what they once believed
do not cry out.

Houses don't warn you when they weaken.

They hold the weather
until the beams rot from the inside.

Monster in the Mirror

She lives behind the glass.
She is what was made
when I could not survive gently.

Built from sleepless nights
and prayers that went unanswered,
from the breathless space
after the screams.

Her spine is made of guilt.
She whispers,
    "You are not worth saving."

For a while,
I believed her.

I used to call her monster.
Now I understand:
she is what torment looked like
wearing my face.

that version is not the woman i am.

i step away from the mirror.

i am not monstrous.

Brilliantly Rearranged

I am not one
but a house with many rooms.
Some walls still wear childhood wallpaper,
others are marked by grief.

Each door guards a version of me.

The betrayal wasn't in what was done.
It was in how I had to lose myself
to survive.

Something took root in me.
Not PTSD.
No.
Those letters are far too clean.

The shadow in my chest,
the echo that tastes like iron
and sounds like my name
said wrong,
shakes the pictures off the walls.

One hides.
One fights.

One tells jokes at parties.
One wears what is not hers.
One still thinks it's her fault.

Inside this skin,
there are rooms that only open
when the air grows tense,
when a sound becomes a trap.

Even now,
I go on.

Together,
we carry each other
through morning.

I do not ask for repair.
Only recognition.

That I am not broken,
        just brilliantly rearranged.

i wonder who you see
when you look at me.

II
THE UNINVITED

innocence dies slowly.

you lose some
when you see
what people are capable of.

you lose the rest
when you realize
you are not set apart.

you knew the parts of me

i kept hidden

and wore them

like party conversation.

Friendships

You sat across from me,
nodding, smiling.
Holding my sins in your palms
like receipts.

I would have died for you.
I would've sworn you innocent.
And I believed
you would do the same.

Traitor

I wasn't just betrayed,
I was auctioned off.

Confessions, tears, trust,
sold cheap
for the price
of a better narrative.

You took our ride-or-die loyalty
and left it bleeding in the street.

And the cruelest part,
something in me
goes looking for you anyway.

Not the traitor you became.
The friend
you pretended to be.

i would've burned cities
for you

you wouldn't even
burn bridges.

lies outlive apologies.

i wasn't naïve.

i was loyal.

and loyalty

is dangerous

around people

who mistake it for weakness.

Waiting for the Moment

Love was never given freely.
It came with unwritten conditions.

Be easier.
Be grateful.
Do not ask for much.

So I trimmed my needs
down to something small enough
to keep.

I learned
how to make myself necessary.

How to be the one
who understood,
who forgave,
who waited.

People remained
as long as I abandoned
the parts of me that needed too much.

i abandoned parts of myself
again and again
just to make sure
someone would keep choosing me.

maybe the damage wasn't
just what you did.

maybe it was
what i did to myself.

ignoring my own breaking.
calling pain passion.
choosing fire over absence.

because even burning
felt better
than becoming invisible.

i know the taste of it

too well

to call it a stranger.

Bulletproof

I made altars of men.

Bodies touched
without ever knowing me.

I called destruction
control.

Called it protection.
Called it freedom.
Called myself bulletproof.

Built a ritual
of my own undoing.

Powder cut across the counter.
A shot glass slick in my hand.

I said I needed no one.
I preferred it this way.

That was a fucking lie.

Take a Bow

It knows the curated smile,
the steady voice,
the calm ingrained in my movements.

It also knows how I falter
beneath the humming yellow light
where the clock
counts everything.

Afterward I sit there knowing
I traded tomorrow
for ten minutes without myself.

My heartbeat kicks **against the dark.**
I whisper I won't do this again,
knowing I will.

Bitter White

I swallow them whole,
bitter-coated,
waiting for relief
that never arrives.

I have mistaken drugs
for relief.

Judgment slips beneath the skin.
The pills promise numbness.
The pills promise escape.

Everything remains muted, waiting,
but fully intact.

I live between the tainted
and what still clings there.

Just present,
inside a body
that remembers all too well.

i tell myself
it is medicine.

but somewhere deeper

i know
the truth.

Medicine & Poison

Loneliness knows my habits
better than anyone,
like an old companion
who never asks questions
because it already knows the answers.

I lay it out carefully,
like something sacred.
I tell people I'm fine.
I post filtered proof.
I have perfected
appearing intact.

Left alone,
the illusion buckles.
The ringing in my ears
blends into the emptiness around me
until I can no longer tell
which one is speaking.

midnight has a shape.

it sits beside me
when this apartment grows watchful
and the corners begin listening.

there are things that only wake in darkness.

scars that still remember
half-buried prayers
the pull of poison
i once called comfort.

i forget the taste of daybreak.

the sharpness of color.

the reach of my voice.

i sink

deeper

until even absence

forgets me.

Held by Absence

The distance between me and relief
keeps getting smaller.

My reflection in the black TV screen
looks back at me,
but I'm already gone.
Pupils blown wide with ache,
like someone waiting for a train
on an empty track.
I think about calling someone.
I follow every tangent
further from myself.

And when it hits,
there's that second,
that thin, cruel second
where everything blurs
and my mind stops screaming.

For a moment, I feel held,
but it isn't love.

I almost cry from
the mercy of it.
But mercy is brief.
Mercy always leaves.

III

SMOKE & MIRRORS

"Promise, Promise"

When I met you,
you told me:

You are enough.
You are safe with me.
I could never hurt you.
I will never leave you.
There is no one else.
You're family.
To me,
you will always be beautiful.

You lied.

Good Morning Texts

Men like you
do not build.
They borrow.
They devour.
They leave.

The first morning
you did not text,
I checked twice.
The second,
I told myself
you were busy.

By the third,
I understood.
There would be
no more good morning texts.

i check my phone
one last time.
the screen is a desert.

i used to wait with hope.
now i wait out of habit,
like muscle memory
for ghosts.

tongues sweet as
Orange Jubilee

gone sour

against my neck
my chest
my thighs.

some feasted.

some bruised me
delicately.

Passing Through

I gave myself to you.
Legs parted.
Lips worn soft.
Mind exposed.
Heart left unguarded.

I loved you
beyond what was asked of me.
Mind and flesh
resting in you
like they had somewhere to belong.

I held you in a place of reverence.
Pity.
To you,
I was just passing through.

Laid Bare

You didn't knock.
You walked right in
like the last one did,
fingers already certain
of the map.

You saw warmth
read it as weakness.
As if tenderness
were not the first place
I learned pain.

I gave you every version of me,
carefully plated.
Desperation dressed as dinner.
Loneliness in lace.

Kiss It Better

Kisses,
pink,
parted,
practiced.

I mistook mouths for meaning,
tongues for truth.
Their tenderness
was a velvet rope
leading straight
to a cage.

I will not become
a sermon
on someone else's lips.

Navy Blue

That night you drove too fast
through red lights and empty intersections,
laughing like nothing could touch you.

I remember gripping the passenger door,
pretending I trusted you.
Your music rattled the windows
until the whole car shook.

You liked the engine loud.
I liked you louder.
I gasped and you told me not to worry.
So I learned to go quiet.

Offering apologies
before you asked for them.
Every lie came dressed as a joke.
Every warning sign
I painted navy blue.

Notions

You discarded me
like a sketch,
something glanced at
and left behind.

You made it seem
like I was everything,
while you played games
I was never meant to win.

My enemy
was your friend.
She held your phone,
your passwords.

While I held
every word you said,
every move you made,
every look you gave.
Grasping at the possibility
that you would
be mine.

Someone Like You

It happens in an instant.
Your face alters.
Not cruelty. Not indifference.
Something beyond either.
A hollowness that enters quietly,
as though a thought
has unsealed a hidden chamber
behind your eyes.

I have pushed myself
into a heart already **haunted**.
Someone unfinished in you.
I feel it
in the pause before your touch,
as if reaching for me
requires burying her memory.

You never speak her name.
But she is there,
between us,
all the same.

Doll Parts

My imagination fed on
echoes of what we once were.
I told myself it was nothing.
A phase.
A mood.
A misunderstanding.

But there were others just like me.
I saw it clearly,
yet I stood there,
a doll balanced in your palm,
posed in a dollhouse.

Identical compartments.
Shared plastic heels
and cracked tiaras.

I thought we were singular.
I was only inventory.
And you,
a collector
of pretty things
that never belonged to you.

Your Jacket Pocket

I removed my heart
and slipped it into your jacket pocket,
between cigarettes and loose coins.
It continued beating.
You never noticed.

You carried it
through crowded bars, unfamiliar doorways,
through mornings that had no memory of me.

Sometimes I imagined
you would reach inside and discover it there.
Your fingers were always occupied
with finding something easier to ignite.

I didn't lose myself.
I cut myself open
for someone already setting fire
to everyone around him.

the loneliness of missing you
has chattering teeth.
it curls beneath the blankets
where you should be.

i mistook

being chosen

for being kept.

Addicted to the Fall

I didn't miss you.
I missed the fall.

The split second
before impact
when everything narrowed
and I could pretend
this was destiny
instead of damage.

You were velocity.
A pull I never resisted.
We did not build.
We accelerated.

My bed does not remember you.
It remembers friction.
I kept calling momentum
fate.

The fall was the addiction.

And every time we fell,
I called it fate
because admitting
I loved the danger
would have required
stopping.

no one fears the fire itself.

only the impulse
to touch
what could consume them.

IV
ELECTRIC NIGHTS

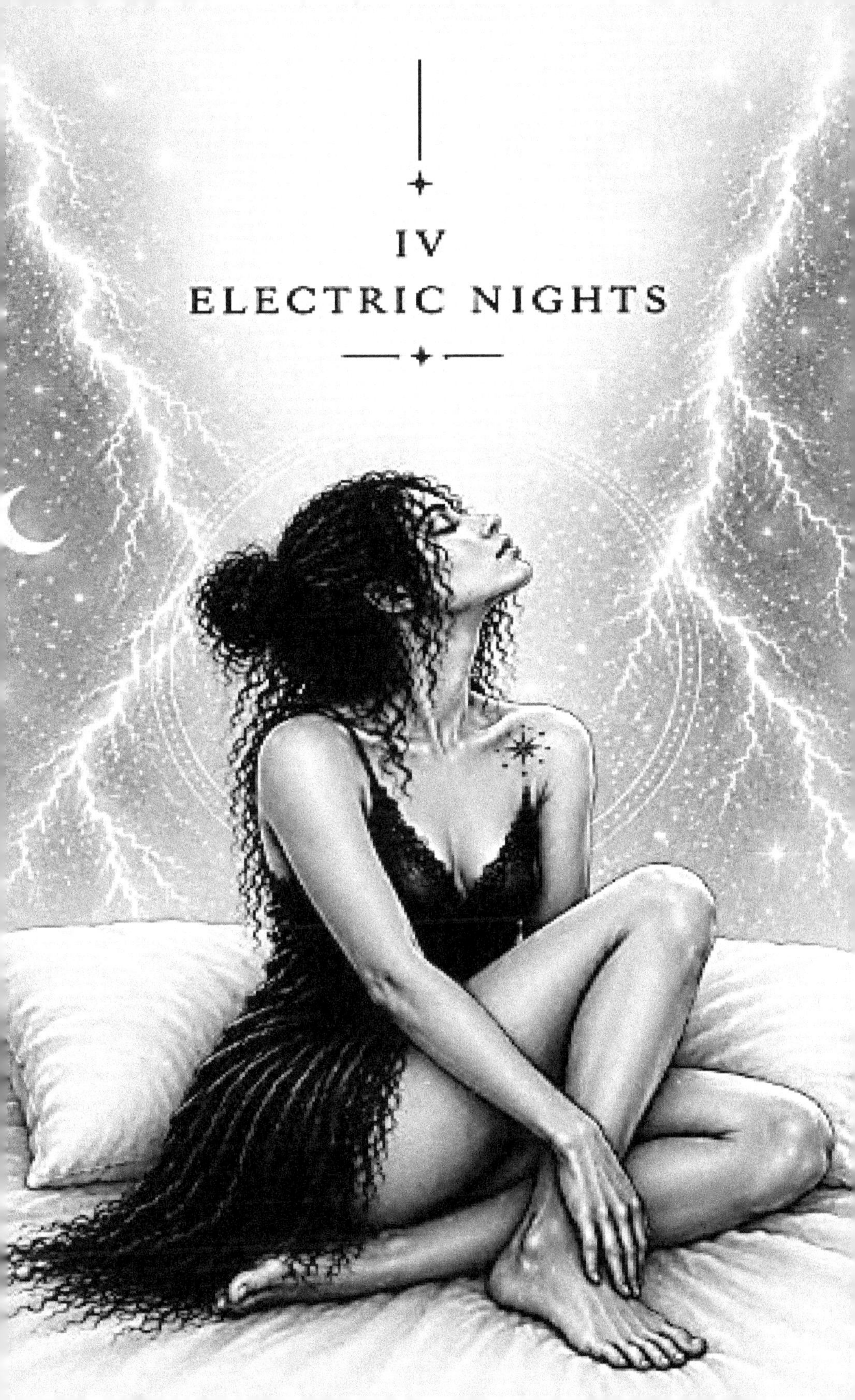

you didn't feel new
you felt remembered.
in some way dangerous.

and somehow
in all of my fear
i welcomed that
as safety.

Mr. E

You appeared
like lightning.
A hundred voices
vanished
when you walked in.

And every time
I unraveled.
Words dissolved
before I could speak them.

I found myself tracing the pulse
of your Adam's apple,
searching for proof
you were made of ordinary things.

Avalanche

The first time I saw you,
something in me surrendered.
Like an avalanche.

My throat dried to dust,
every word abandoned me,
and language,
my oldest companion,
turned traitor.

You moved through the crowd
inevitable as gravity.
I desired you.
The warmth of your nearness,
the proof of you
close enough to breathe in.

Every instinct in me said
this was dangerous.
That love,
after this moment,
would never be simple again.

Fated

It felt cinematic.
Like a dream
stepping into the room,
alive.

The moment you looked at me
like I was something worth studying.

It was slow at first.

I eased into you
like I was stepping
into cool water.

Before realizing
I could no longer touch bottom.

You felt familiar.

Not because we were meant to be,
but because you spoke
to the parts of me
I left unguarded.

I called recognition destiny.
Intensity for truth.

I knew everything
was about to change.
And it did.

across a crowded room
it felt as though fate
had written itself
into our silhouettes.

i stood there
pretending to exist

while inside
whole galaxies
collapsed.

Too Close to Touch

I watched you
more than I should have,
the lines across your palms,
the measured control in your fingers,
and that impossible hair.

I wondered how many lovers
your hands had touched.

I was mesmerized,
alarmed, even,
by how fast it happened.

We only ever had fragments of time,
stolen glances,
half-formed sentences.
Suspended.

But it was enough.
Enough to forget
how careful I had promised to be.

You stood too close,
and something in me
gave way.

I imagined what would happen
if you ever touched me too.

I shivered at the thought of you.

I had said I was above this.
Past this recklessness.

Then you looked at me,
and something deeper answered
before I could stop it.

Boy in the Magazine

There you are,
leaning against that yard fence,
sunglasses pushed back,
looking entirely too comfortable.

I catch myself studying
your imperfect tattoo lines,
tracing them like constellations
I was never close enough to touch.

I sit inside my afflictions,
thinking about how easily
that could be me beside you.

How easily
I could become
where your evenings end.

Instead,
your chain rests against your chest.
Your rings know your fingers
better than I ever could.

Even the fence
gets your weight.

God,
how easily
I become jealous of metal.

Almost Mine

I had a habit
of pursuing what was already taken.
I don't chase empty palms.
I chase the ones already held.

There is something about the boundary
that pulls me closer,
the forbidden risk,
the almost.
The way desire narrows
when it isn't allowed.

I told myself
it was accidental.
That I didn't know.

I saw the ring.
The history.
The way your phone flips over.
But I knew, with you.
It was not to steal.
Only to win.

Captive

I wanted you.
Not in another lifetime.
Not in fantasy.

And you let me want you.
You leaned in.
You lingered.
You were taken.
And I knew it.

I was not innocent in it.
But don't pretend
you didn't feel it too.

I leaned in.

You kept me
captive.

Heat

We met at the threshold
of what we knew was wrong.

You didn't touch me at first.
We called it restraint.
It was *anticipation.*

When you finally reached for me,
it was fleeting.

It was heat.

And suddenly,
there was a before
and an after.

Breathe Me

I needed one more night.
Not love.
Impact.

The kind that loosens caution
and makes you forget
who you were before the door closed.

We didn't promise anything.
We burned.
You touched me
like you were writing a song.

For a moment,
I believed you.
But morning is honest.
And daylight keeps records.

I gave you
the parts of me
meant for permanence.
I had been
the celebration.
Not the future.

Drinks Sin Deep

Wine on bare skin.

Kisses taken

as if time were running out.

The room held us,

the ceiling indifferent.

Everything cooled.

The sheets creased.

I sit with it sometimes,

the music.

Proof

that it happened.

Beautiful Boy

The world had already decided
our future.

You looked exactly
like someone
I had spent my whole life
asking God for.

You were not perfect.

It was beyond that.

You felt
like an eclipse.
The kind that only comes once.

You were intoxicating.
Not because you tried to be.

Because being near you
bent
the world around us.

I replayed every moment
the way someone rewatches
the same music video.

Not to remember.

To feel it all over again.

At night,
I watched you sleep.

Sometimes,
when the room was the only witness,
I would whisper,
my beautiful boy.

I had waited so long
for something
everyone said
would never happen.

For a moment,
I was the greatest.
I had believed God's plan
before anyone else did.

My faith
had outrun
the world.

Everyone remembers
how stories ended.

I remember
how impossible ours was
to begin.

nothing after this moment
would ever belong to me again.

whatever i was
before you
was already gone.

V

DYING TO LOVE

i called you everything
i ever wanted
long before i knew
who you were.

All I Ever Wanted

It started to hurt.
Like actual pain.
Not metaphor.

How my chest locked tight.
Like something was always
about to break.

I was already bracing.

You'd say something.
Do something.

And I felt it land.

I was disheveled in you.

Not just undone.
Misplaced.

Like I kept placing myself
inside the wrong story
and calling it destiny.

I kept insisting
you were everything
I ever wanted.

If I said it enough times,
it began to sound true.

Circa

We became the dream of us,
something we once believed
was forever
because forever felt possible.

I remember you,
my high school sweetheart,
all laughter and reckless light.

You were the one
who turned ordinary days
into something worth keeping.

Until that safety
gave way to uncertainty.

I loved you
in the spaces you were leaving,
holding onto the version of us
that was already gone.

The weight of holding on
became heavier
than letting go.

And I will keep
the piece of who we were
that taught me how to love.

We were no longer the people we met.
We had become the hindrance
to the dream of us.

i was never foolish.
i confused pleasure
for permanence.
you left
as beautiful things often do
without apology.

you were gone
long before.

when i'm done

i'm done.

you don't get

two chances

to make me feel small.

well…

i've made exceptions.

To Wish Impossible Things

There are days
when the sequence feels rigged.

I am pulled back
to the moment
just before you left.

As if disbelief
were a room
I keep re-entering.

I offer this:
a cracked porcelain cup
ringed with old stains,
left on the counter
long after it should have been cleared.

Between being wanted
and being left
there are only
different versions
of captivity.

Endure

I stayed
in the illusion
that "real"
was supposed to feel like this.

Like enduring
meant receiving.

I thought
this was love.

But love was never meant
to make you flinch,
never meant
to make you disappear
just to keep it.

You were *not* everything
I ever wanted.

love does not ask you
to look away.

it does not leave you
unraveled
calling it love.

it does not cut into you
and then ask
why you're bleeding.

i think that's when i knew
love had left us

long before
we ever walked away.

i stopped reaching for you.
you didn't notice.

Vestiges

I begged in the quiet ways,
by waiting,
by remembering
what you forgot,
by keeping the bed
tilted toward your side.

You left in increments:
a missed call,
a delayed reply,
a hand that no longer reached first.

We felt it
before we could admit it,
your attention
finding a rhythm
that did not include us.

We got good at pretending.
Mascara was never thick enough
to survive the night.
Messages typed
and erased.

You called it distance.
I called it temporary.
It was already over.

Sweet Air

Sitting between us are
conversations that never landed,
apologies that sounded right
but passed straight through me,
the silence
that outlasted love.

You moved through the room,
setting things back in place,
as if alignment could steady us.

Sweetness in the air,
as if kindness alone
could undo what had shifted.

But the air held
everything we refused to say.

And somehow that
hurt more
than all the ways
we used to come apart.

we were two people
standing in the same room
eating off plates
that had already gone cold.

resentment begins as a wound
but grows like a vine.

by the time you notice it
it has climbed
around everything.

Love Me Clean

Growing
in the darkened corners
of a love
that once felt clean.

The black bloom of mold.

Fed by
a word misplaced,
a hurt left too long,
an apology
that never arrived.

You tell yourself
it's fine.

Wipe the surface,
light a jasmine-scented candle,
open a window,
but underneath,
it lives.

Miss Your Face

I miss how
your name
tasted in my mouth.

The version of myself
that existed in your gaze.

You saw me
the way no one else did.

Not who I pretended to be.
Not who the world decided I was.

You found
the woman beneath
all the hiding.

Somehow, I forgot
I had ever needed
to protect myself.

Before our laughter
became something
we remembered
instead of shared.

There is a violence to
letting go.

Remnants

I walk around carrying these parts of you,
these remnants of you.

Not memories.
Residue.

I am suspicious of the wind.
It moves like smoke,
sudden, invasive,
and impossible to hold.

Spent embers gather
in the pocket of my peacoat.
Gray dust
caught in the seams,
refusing to brush free.

In my bed
the sheets remember
where we burnt through the night.

The scent of you clings
to my hair,
to the collar of your old band T-shirts.

I walk around carrying parts of you.
These remnants of you.

i kept holding on

because letting go

meant accepting

i deserved better.

Up in Flames

You didn't love me.
You loved being adored.
And I was convenient,
until I wasn't.

You were sweet at first.
Then the flames turned blue.

I wore black when I said "I do,"
a ceremony soaked in irony,
anointed in hindsight.

As for the girl
who once would've wept for you,
she's gone.

I buried her,
said no farewell,
burned the dress,
and walked away
without your last name.

the wound was never
that you left
or what you did.

the wound was
that i stayed.

i stayed long enough
to start abandoning myself.

every ending
requires a burial
not every burial
requires a grave.

VI

FORGED

I chose me.

I built.

I became.

NO ONE GETS TO
TELL ME WHO I AM AGAIN.

Shedding Skin

Death is not always a coffin,
not always a pulse abandoning flesh.

Sometimes,
death is the slow collapse
of a relationship
that once held you upright.

Sometimes,
death is turning away
from the person your past insisted you be,
a shedding of skin
you outgrew years ago.

Old patterns decay,
old identities split open,
the voice that ruled your mind
is stripped of its crown.

Entire lifetimes vanish
inside a single decision.

A former self
is lowered into the soil of yesterday.

But here is the truth people miss:
death is also a crossing.

It cuts the cord
between who you carried for years
and who is climbing out of the wreckage.

Every ending
burns the field clean.

Yet from the ash,
something long forgotten
pushes through
the callous dark.

No longer following,
but leading,
it steps forward
and begins again.

Indigo Sway

It is hard to love me.
To witness the sway,
indigo moving through indigo.

The shift,
the way affection hardens
into something volatile
without warning.

What lives inside me
is not gentle water.
Not everyone survives
this depth.

Uninvited

All of you were
blistered-out men,
empty coats
left on rusted nails.

Every one of you
took something,
a slice of heart,
a patch of skin,
parts of me I once called strength.

You drank from my trust,
rinsed your guilt in my forgiveness,
and left
with my shame
still clinging to your teeth.

I kept sweeping up
what you dropped,
buttons, excuses.

The mark of your grip
pressed into the walls I built.

After a while
I stopped asking
why the door was always open.

Not every knock
earns an answer.

Smoke

You left me, cruelly.
Cast me aside.
Threw out my things as if I was nothing.
Then returned to her like I had been a fever
you sweated out in secret.

Boxed my dresses.
Cleared away my toothbrush.
Scrubbed my presence
from the bathroom mirror.

I stood there holding the outline
of what we were,
realizing I loved a man
who rearranged history with a straight face.

You went back to her,
virtue restored.
Like she was marble,
while I was smoke.

But
smoke lingers.

You called.
You needed to see me,
your lady in red returned.
You opened the door
and pulled me in.

The linens didn't hesitate.
Neither did you.
But I wasn't there to be kept.
I was there
to ruin your peace.

When I dressed,
I moved slowly.
Lipstick deliberate.
Heels whispering across the floor.

I left one cigarette
on your nightstand.
My shade pressed into the filter
like a signature.

You once treated me
as if I were nothing.
But *nothing*
doesn't leave a mark.

Even now,
after all her questions,
both of you
remember the smoke.

you tried
to unmake me.

i survived
in spite of you.

Hindsight

You said,
"God will forgive me."

I told you
I never would.

You brought me an apology
in the same fists that struck me.

I hope my moving on
tastes like rust in your mouth.

You thought
I'd be waiting.

Little boy,
I already redecorated
my life without you.

I scraped the illusion of you
from the ceiling,
washed the stains away,
and erased your face
from every room.

You no longer exist
with me.

what you took

taught me

what is mine.

i will never let myself

be taken like that again.

keep counting apologies
like coins.

we will never be even.

the strongest boundaries
are rarely spoken.

they are simply upheld.

i refused to accept erasure
as the cost of being heard

i remain
uncontained.

Heart Shaped Glasses

I am not your wreckage.
Not your confession.
Not your refuge
where you came,
cowardly,
to feel briefly forgiven.

You scattered my worth,
my confidence,
my anger.

Instead
I gathered myself,
thread by thread,
stitch by stitch.

This time
I choose.

No pleading for affection.
No shrinking
to fit someone else's comfort.

I will let you sit
with the version of me
you never get to see.

I will not bend toward anyone
who treated me
like an option.

I took off
my heart-shaped glasses.

My love didn't disappear.
Only the people
who never deserved it.

the most dangerous thing

i ever became

was a woman

certain of her own worth.

i did not become powerful
because life was kind.

i became powerful
because it wasn't.

i learned early
that volume unsettles people
that fire makes people nervous

that a woman
who does not fold
is difficult to hold.

Unapologetic

They suggested containment:
less intensity,
less of myself.

I did not comply.

I could not breathe
any smaller.

Let them shift in their seats.
Let them call it a flaw.

I was never excess.
I was pressure
without apology.

Sweet Nothings

"Tell me something," she says.

"You are ugly," he says.

"Tell me something," she says.

"You are nothing," he says.

"Tell me something true," she says.

"You are useless," he says.

"Tell me something true," she says.

"I won't miss you," he says.

As she walks away from him,
for the last time, he asks:

"How could you do this to me?"

She continues walking.

He calls out to her:

"Tell me something true."

She pauses.
A smile curls at the corner of her mouth.

She turns to him and says:

"I'll miss you."

Mercy

I forgive you.
Not because you asked.
Not because you earned it.

But because I am tired
of dragging your choices behind me.

Because my heart is done
revisiting the moment
everything changed.

Bitterness is an anchor.
I have carried it long enough.

My loyalty
was never the mistake.
You just handled it poorly.

I release you.
Not to return to the house
you set on fire,
but to leave
without **the scent of soot**
clinging to me.

I refuse to be a monument
to what you broke.

my peace

is no longer negotiable.

your depth is not darkness.

the right people
will know the difference.
they will see it
for what it is
and walk toward it
without fear.

Water Against Iron

I was not ruined.
I was heated.

What struck me
met resistance.

What burned
did not consume.
It refined.

I am no longer
a house with open doors.

I am the iron
beneath it.

The flood was relentless.
I was inevitable.

The haze did not blind me.
It taught me
how to see through it.

You took me for
something breakable.

I was only becoming.

Now,
what reaches for me
meets resistance.

I do not hold the weather.
I make it.

red on my lips.

leather at my back.

i have outlived every name

they tried to pin to me.

i belong to movement.

to horizon.

if they ask who i am

tell them.

Wearing Me Well

It was never protection.
Only proximity.

That exquisite scar,
fading now,
but no less mine.

I built cathedrals from your assurances,
spired and ornate,
hollow at the center.

You were not my ruin.
You were my revelation.

The architecture survives,
though the tenant is gone.

The dark lives here.
Not as shadow.
Not as punishment.
But as part of what I became.

And I wear it well.

Maker of Men

I have made men.
They came to me
untested.
All appetite and ache.

I wove them
from hunger and heat,
gave them strength
where there was none.
I built them
bone by bone,
filled their veins
with my passion.

They left
taller.
Louder.
Certain.

They stood
on my conviction.

Every time,
I watched them go.

Some called me dangerous.
Some called me magic.

They forget.

I was never the altar.
I am the forge.

If I am a maker of men,
it is only because
I survived them.

the dark is not temporary.

it has taught me.

it has stood beside every ledger of my life:
rupture, craving, survival
its thumbprint pressed into each.

i have spent too many years
trying to translate it.

it asks for nothing.
neither do i.

To My Beautiful Readers

Some of these poems were born in difficult places. They have traveled with me from adolescence through many seasons of my life. They are part of my story as a survivor. They come from grief, trauma, addiction, depression, and moments when the weight of living felt unbearable.

Some of these poems explore difficult emotions and experiences, including thoughts of suicide and profound emotional pain.

If you see pieces of yourself in these pages, please know you are not alone. If you are struggling, reach for someone. Let another human being carry a corner of the weight with you.

In the United States, call or text 988 to reach the Suicide & Crisis Lifeline.

You are needed. You are loved. You are meant to be here. You are *becoming.* ♥

Thank you for trusting me with your heart.

With love,

Tiffany D.

Recognition

"Brilliantly Rearranged" received ***Third Place*** *in the* ***2026 Mental Health Creative Arts Contest****, a statewide Texas competition hosted by the Texas Institute for Excellence in Mental Health at* ***The University of Texas at Austin****.*

Thank you for walking through these pages with me.

If you found a piece of yourself in these poems, please consider leaving a review on Amazon. Your review helps this book reach others who may need it.

With gratitude,

Tiffany D.

www.ingramcontent.com/pod-product-compliance
Lightning Source LLC
LaVergne TN
LVHW022222200926
848481LV00006B/2070
* 9 7 9 8 9 9 8 6 1 9 1 3 7 *